Rounds About Rounds

Rounds About Rounds

Collected and Edited by

Jane Yolen

Musical Arrangements by

Barbara Green

Illustrated by

Gail Gibbons

Franklin Watts/New York/London/1977

For our children, who are great rounds singers:
Heidi, Adam, and Jason Stemple
Chris and Elizabeth Snyder

round about and round about and round about again

Library of Congress Cataloging in Publication Data

Main entry under title:
Rounds about rounds.

Includes bibliography and index.
SUMMARY: A collection of over seventy old
and new rounds with brief notes about their
origins and piano accompaniment.
1. Glees, catches, rounds, etc. [1. Songs]
I. Yolen, Jane H. II. Green, Barbara S. III.
Gibbons, Gail.
M1495.R835   784'.1   77-7919
ISBN 0-531-00125-3

# Contents

About Rounds *1*
Singing Rounds *4*

All Things Must Perish *6*
Oh, Music, Sweet Music *8*
Now We'll Make the Rafters Ring *10*
Make New Friends *11*
Merrily, Merrily *12*
Viva la Musica *14*
The Bell Doth Toll *16*
White Coral Bells *18*
Little Bells of Westminster *20*
Great Tom Is Cast *21*
Oh, How Lovely Is the Evening *22*
Rose, Rose *24*
Early to Bed *26*
Man's Life's a Vapor *28*
Hey Ho, Nobody's Home *30*
The Wise Men Were but Seven *32*
Seven Great Towns of Greece *34*
Scotland's Burning *36*
French Cathedrals *38*
Turn Again, Whittington *40*
Frère Jacques *42*
Where Is John? *44*
The Ghost of John *46*
Jack, Boy, Ho! *48*
Jane Glover *50*
My Dame Hath *52*
Sandy McNab *54*
Row, Row, Row Your Boat *56*
A Boat, a Boat! *58*

Canoe Round 60
Where Are You Going? 62
Chairs to Mend: I 64
Chairs to Mend: II 66
White Sand and Gray Sand 68
Cherries So Ripe 69
Buy My Dainty Fine Beans 70
Soul Cakes 72
Dame, Lend Me a Loaf 74
Christmas Is Coming 76
Come Follow, Follow 78
Summer Is A-Coming In 80
All Is Silent 84
Kookaburra 86
Thou Poor Bird 88
Why Shouldn't My Goose 90
Donkeys and Carrots 92
Sweetly Sings the Donkey 94
Hey Ho, to the Greenwood 96
Three Blind Mice 98
The Frogs 100
The Sun It Rises 102
Ho! Ev'ry Sleeper Waken 104
Goodnight to You All 106
Shaker Life 108
Shalom Chaverim 110
Dona Nobis Pacem 112
Rounds About Rounds 114

Sources of Rounds 116
Sources of Additional Material 117
Alphabetical List of Rounds 119

Rounds About Rounds

About Rounds

One of the simplest and most popular games is "Follow the Leader." It has been played on city streets and country roads, in school and out, for hundreds of years. And one of the simplest and most popular kinds of singing is also a follow-the-leader game—the singing of rounds.

In the seventeenth and eighteenth centuries, all manner of people sang part songs: lords and ladies in their fine halls, tinkers and coopers and craftsmen at their work, broom sellers and flower girls calling their wares, bell ringers and church singers too. These simple part songs—rounds and catches and canons—were especially well liked. The songs were lively, easy to remember, and a lot of fun.

The round is the simplest of the three. It is a short song with two or more voices, and is to be repeated by each singer several times through. One singer begins, the next comes in at the proper time. The phrases of the song, each the same length, harmonize with one another.

The catch was first just another name for simple rounds. But it developed into a special kind of song with words written in such a way that, when the parts are combined, unexpected meanings emerge. Often these unexpected meanings are quite bawdy.

The canon is the most complicated of the three part songs. The word *canon* comes from the word for *law*. In music over the centuries, many complex and fascinating laws or instructions have been given to the voice or instrument entering second in line, including singing the melody upside down and backwards! In this collection, however, *canon* is synonymous with *round*. It indicates that the second voice, and all those that follow, sing the original melody, entering at regularly spaced intervals.

The paradox of rounds is this: they are counterpointed, or many-voiced. And while rounds are considered the simplest and most innocent form of part singing imaginable, counterpoint has always been regarded as one of the most advanced forms of music.

The first round officially written down and noted was "Sumer Is Icumen In" by a thirteenth-century monk. Nearly a hundred years later,

[1]

the second recorded round is found, "Rowe the Bote, Norman," which we sing today as "Turn Again, Whittington." That is not to say that there were no rounds sung in the interim, just that no records were kept of the songs.

It was in the sixteenth century, however, that many books and plays began to mention "merry songs" and "jolly singing" and even rounds and catches by name. For example, in Shakespeare's play *A Winter's Tale* we hear: "Bear a Part, 'Tis in Three."

However, though the rounds were mentioned, they were not set down musically until a century later. In the seventeenth century, rounds became so popular that Britain, which was known as the "Ringing Isle" because of its many bells, became known also as the "Singing Isle."

Rounds did not remain in Britain, however. They were quickly exported to continental Europe, and soon composers all over Europe were creating part songs or translating them. Eventually the best composers tried their hand at rounds—in different centuries, Bach, Haydn, Mozart, Beethoven—but they were not necessarily any more successful at rounds than commonplace and often anonymous composers at such simple songs.

The earliest collections of rounds were made by Thomas Ravenscroft and David Melvill. *Pammelia,* Ravenscroft's first collection, was published in London in 1609, when he was only seventeen years old. Like many musicians, he was precocious. He brought out a second volume the same year, *Deuteromelia or The Seconde part of Musicks melodie.* And two years later, in 1611, young Ravenscroft put together a third volume, *Melismata.* In 1612, Melvill's *Ane Buik off Roundells* appeared in Edinburgh. (Spelling was still a matter of personal preference rather than rule!) It contained many of the same rounds that were found in Ravenscroft's works. However, since there is no evidence that Melvill knew either Ravenscroft or his books, music scholars feel sure that both men were simply recording rounds and part songs that were already popular in the British Isles.

British kings were overthrown by Puritans and Puritans were succeeded by kings, and the popularity of singing in general—and rounds in particular—was an up-and-down thing. But in the end, "Viva la Musica," rounds lived. And they flourished.

[2]

In fact, in Britain round singing was so popular that *catch clubs* were organized for singing for enjoyment, entertainment, and occasional prizes. They began in the late 1700s and the most famous of them all—the Nobleman's & Gentleman's Catch Club—is still a going concern. It disbanded only once, from 1915 to 1919; then it opened again and this time allowed women to sing in it, too.

Some of the songs in this book of rounds are serious and some are silly, some are lovely and lyrical and some are . . . well, some are not. But whenever I come upon the words of a round that are particularly foolish, I remember George Bernard Shaw's "What's too silly to be said can be sung" and then just open my mouth and sing.

Jane Yolen

Singing Rounds

Making music by yourself is a wonderful experience. Making music with somebody else is an extraordinary experience, and rounds are just the place to start.

Rounds lay invaluable groundwork in early music training. A group of young children that has learned a simple song very well, and is then divided into two groups to sing the same song in canon, is handling the fundamentals upon which all later musical experiences and techniques will be built: rhythmic and melodic independence. The group and the individuals also feel a great sense of fun and satisfaction with what they can do, equally essential ingredients for enjoying music. If the song has been learned well and the groups are large enough, the children have no need to cover their ears in order to sustain their own parts. They begin to live with and hear the intricacies of counterpoint and harmony long before they ever need to analyze them on a conscious level.

With early, simple successes, the children's appetite for more complicated challenges grows, as does their conscious awareness of their independence and interdependence. I was working with a group of eight- and nine-year-olds on a two-part round, which they dearly loved. *They* asked to sing it in four parts; and they themselves set up the musical ground rules that would help them do it well. They did it perfectly, and the feeling of elation in the room at that moment is really what music is all about.

Aesthetically, the color of human voices moving with and against each other is unique. Dissonances that might be grating or harsh on certain instruments become quite special as voices pull against each other or glide on by. However, many rounds lend themselves beautifully to instrumental ensembles, which is something to keep in mind as you use this collection.

Some of the unlikeliest rounds (by title or text) have the most intriguing harmonic texture. "The Ghost of John" is indeed haunting. So take the time to explore them all. And experiment with them, too. We have indicated several rounds that are lovely when sung against each

[4]

other. You will find more. Try adding or taking away voices in a given round, and varying the dynamics of each singing part.

The rounds vary in their complexity. As you choose them and experiment with them, think carefully about the abilities of the groups that will be singing them. Knowing that they've done it well is the key to anyone wanting to touch another piece of singing music ever again!

Why does a book of rounds need piano accompaniments? These are only aids to help in teaching the songs to a group. Unless, of course, you have nobody to sing with at the moment, and would like to explore the songs and spend time with them on your own. The accompaniments should *never* be used when the songs are sung in parts; for the voices make the richest music you can find, and the piano will only obscure it.

At the end of a happy round fest, you have a roomful of people loving the wonder of the music, themselves, and each other . . . an experience that exists only through sharing. One cannot have it alone.

Enjoy!

Barbara Green

All Things Must Perish

*This is a two-part canon originally in German that
is very popular in British and American schools.*

With gentle authority

All things must per - ish from un - der the sky.
Him - mel und Er - de müs - sen ver - gehn;

Mu - sic a - lone shall live,
a - ber die Mu - si - ci

Mu - sic a - lone shall live, Mu - sic a - lone shall live, nev - er to die.
a - ber die Mu - si - ci, a - ber die Mu - si - ci, bleib - en be - stehn.

Since singing is so good a thing,
I wish all men would learne to sing!

William Byrd

Since singing is so good a thing,
Women, too, should learn to sing.

Anon

Persons should unite in song,
So come, dear friends, and sing along.

J.Y. and B.G.

Oh, Music, Sweet Music

This three-part round was
first sung in nineteenth-century Britain.

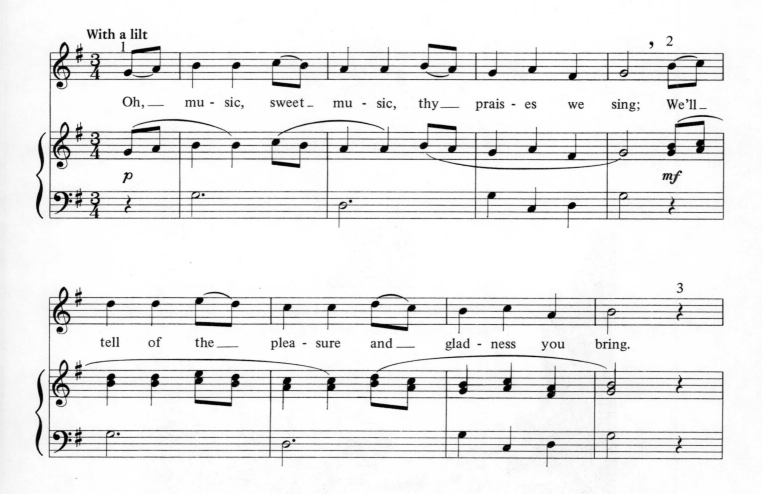

Oh,__ mu - sic, sweet__ mu - sic, thy__ prais - es we sing; We'll__ tell of the __ plea - sure and __ glad - ness you bring.

Mu - sic, mu - sic, glad - ness you bring.

James Green, a shoemaker of Bronygarth, was on his way to a festive gathering one evening when he met an infuriated bull in a narrow lane. Hoping to escape attack, he hastily climbed into a tree. The bull, however, took up a determined position beneath the branches, obviously resolved not to lose his man. The shoemaker, thinking longingly of the merry evening he was about to miss, decided to try the charms of music upon the savage beast. Taking his crwth [an early plucking/bowing instrument] out of his bag, he struck up a favorite tune. To his surprise, the animal turned and fled. "Stop! Stop!" cried James, his wounded pride overcoming his fears, "I'll change the tune!"

From *Old English Instruments of Music* by Francis W. Galpin

Now We'll Make the Rafters Ring

This four-part round was written in the eighteenth century.
The composer is unknown.

Now we'll make the raf - ters ring While we all this round will sing.

Sing, sing, what shall I sing?
The cat's run away with the pudding string!
Do, do, what shall I do?
The cat has bitten it quite in two!

Nursery rhyme, early nineteenth century

Make New Friends

*This is an English round also popular in America and
often sung in camps or at the end of Brownie Scout meetings.*

Make new friends but keep the old; One is sil-ver and the oth-er gold.

He is no friend who in thine hour of pride
Brags of his love and calls himself thy kin.
He is a friend who hales his fellow in,
And clangs the door upon the wolf outside.

Saadi, thirteenth-century Persian poet

Merrily, Merrily

An eighteenth-century
English round in four voices.

hear them play, O'er hill and dale and far a - way!

Tom he was a piper's son,
He learnt to play when he was young,
And all the tune that he could play
Was "Over the hills and far away. . . ."

Nursery song,
seventeenth century

[13]

Viva la Musica

Michael Praetorius, who lived from 1571 to 1621,
was a German composer and music historian.
He wrote the song in Latin.
It means "Long live music" or "Music lives."

MICHAEL PRAETORIUS

Music has charms to soothe a savage breast,
To soften rocks, or bend a knotted oak.

    William Congreve,
    from *The Mourning Bride*

The Bell Doth Toll

*This happy three-part round is anonymous
and comes from America.*

The bell doth toll, Its ech - oes roll, I know the sound full

well. I love its ring - ing, For it calls to sing - ing with its

bim, bim, bim, bom bell. Bim _____

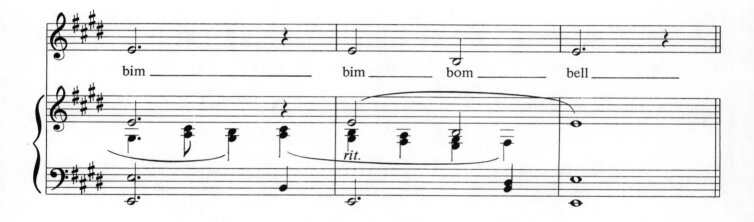

bim _____ bim _____ bom _____ bell _____

To call the fold to church in time,
    We chime.
When joy and mirth are on the wing,
    We ring.
When we lament a departed soul,
    We toll.

    Old bell rhyme

White Coral Bells

*This traditional two-part round is American,
a version of an old
English round from several centuries ago.
It is a popular camp song.*

That will hap-pen on-ly when the fair-ies sing.

Little Dawn Bird was sent on a mission to the top of the great mountain. Fearing she would lose her way, she took white pebbles in her beak. At each step, she placed a pebble on a green leaf to mark her path. While Little Dawn Bird was on the mountaintop, the white pebbles took root and became tiny bells. Little Dawn Bird easily found her way down the mountain, following the tinkling sound of the white bells.

Cherokee Indian legend
about the lily of the valley

Little Bells of Westminster

*The most famous clock tune
in the world is "Westminster Chimes."
The whole tune is played by the bells
of the British Houses of Parliament
in London every hour.*

The lit - tle bells of West - min - ster go ding, dong, ding, dong, dong.

Tune played by Westminster Chimes.

Great Tom Is Cast

Great Tom, the famous bell at Oxford University in England,
rings out curfew at nine o'clock every night with 101 strokes.
Many songs and stories have been written about it.
This three-part round was composed by Dean Henry Aldrich,
who taught at the university in the late 1600s.

DEAN HENRY ALDRICH

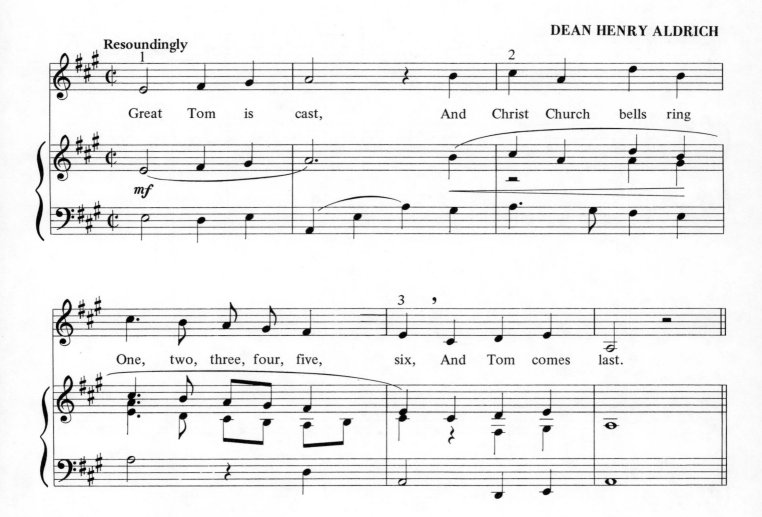

Oh, How Lovely Is the Evening

In Germany this lovely round is not nearly as popular
as in its English version, though it began as a German canon,
"Die Abendglocken," less than two centuries ago.

Sweet and flowing

Oh, how love-ly is the eve - ning,

O wie wohl ist mir am A - bend,

is the eve - ning, When the bells are

mir am A - bend, Wenn zur Ruh' die

sweet - ly ring - ing, sweet - ly ring - ing, Ding,
Glock - en läut - en, Glock - en läut - en, Bim,

mf

dong,   ding,   dong,   ding,   dong.
bam,   *bim,*   *bam,*   *bim,*   *bam.*

loco   *pp*

I am the voice of life:
I call you:
Come and pray.

**Inscription on a
German bell from
the Middle Ages**

Rose, Rose

This lovely anonymous four-part round is from England.

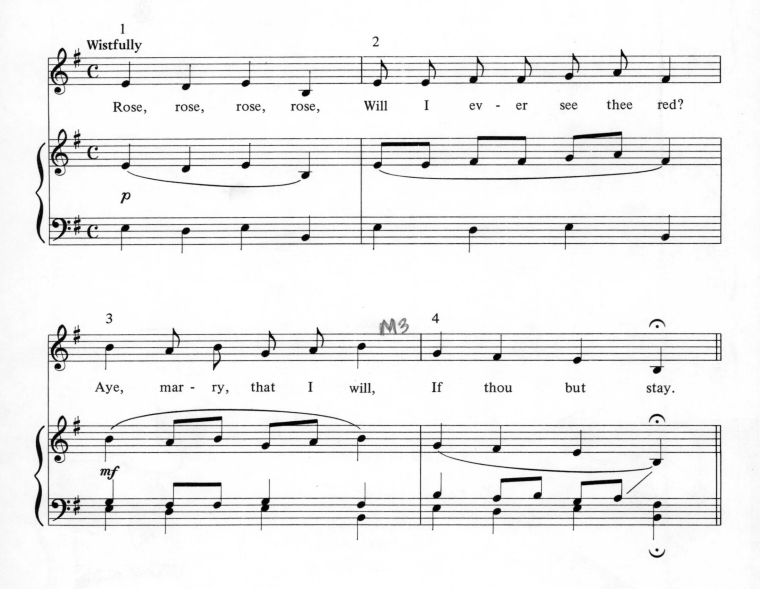

Rose, rose, rose, rose, Will I ev - er see thee red?

Aye, mar - ry, that I will, If thou but stay.

Go, lovely Rose!
Tell her, that wastes her time and me,
That now she knows,
When I resemble her to thee,
How sweet and fair she seems to be.

Edmund Waller

Try singing this with "Thou Poor Bird,"
simultaneously or in canon; and in
canon with "Hey Ho, Nobody's Home"
("Rose, Rose" entering on the
second measure of "Hey Ho").

[25]

Early to Bed

*This three-part American round is based on
Benjamin Franklin's famous proverb from
Poor Richard's Almanac, which in itself came
from John Clarke's Paroemiologia (1639).*

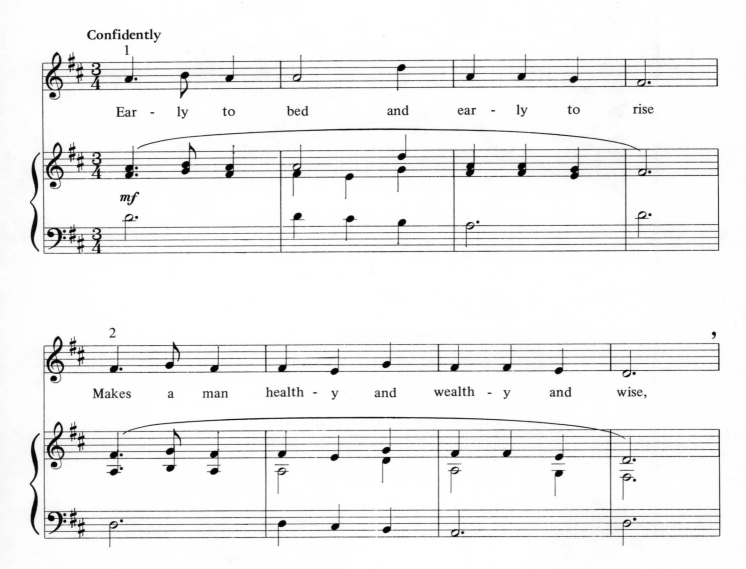

Ear - ly to bed and ear - ly to rise

Makes a man health - y and wealth - y and wise,

Wise, health-y, and wealth - y.

Early to bed and early to rise,
and you won't meet many prominent people.

George Ade

Early to bed and early to rise
And your girl goes out with other guys.

American slang saying

Man's Life's a Vapor

*This charming three-part round is from England. Notice how
the music goes down and down and down at the right moments.*

I am a maid of constant sorrow,
I've seen trouble all my days,
I'm going back to West Virginia,
A place where I was born and raised.

American folk song

Hey Ho, Nobody's Home

*A popular camp song, this five-part round was first
set down in the English songbook* Pammelia *in 1609.*

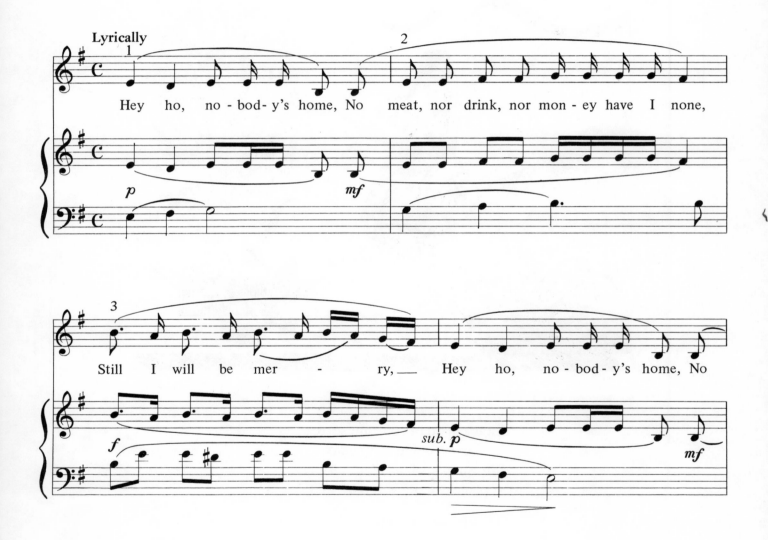

meat, nor drink, nor mon- ey have I none, Still I will be mer — ry,

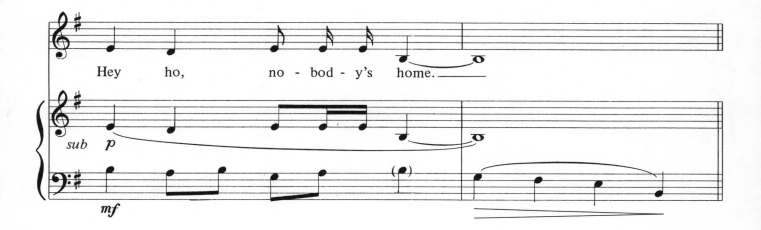

Hey ho, no - bod - y's home.

This song can be sung with three others:
"Thou Poor Bird" and "Soul Cakes"; and
"Rose, Rose," entering in canon, after
the first measure of "Hey Ho." In fact,
you will find the left hand playing two
of those songs in this accompaniment.

The Wise Men Were but Seven

*William Lawes, who lived during the first half
of the seventeenth century, wrote this three-part round.*

WILLIAM LAWES

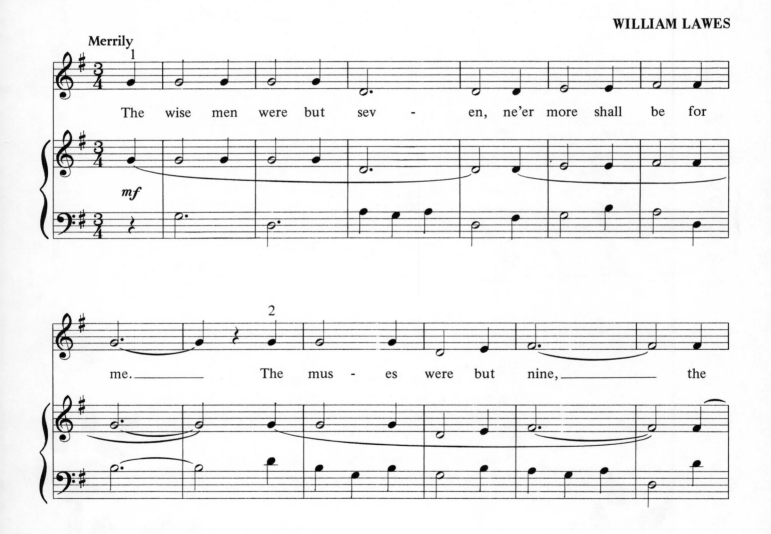

The wise men were but sev - en, ne'er more shall be for
me._____ The mus - es were but nine,_____ the

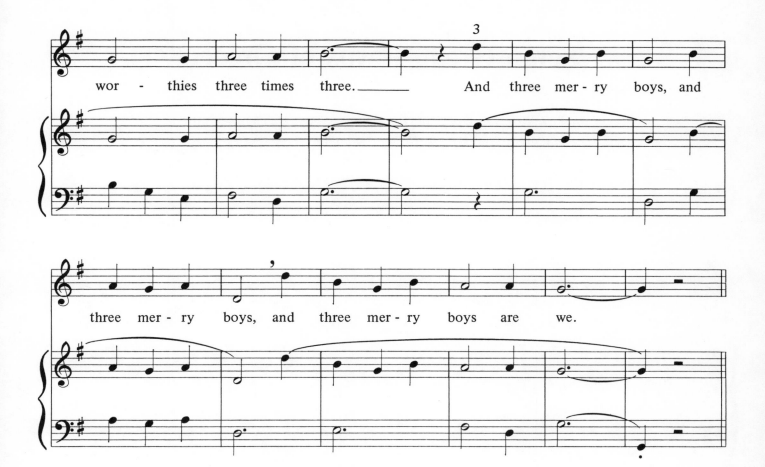

wor - thies three times three._____ And three mer - ry boys, and

three mer - ry boys, and three mer - ry boys are we.

The muses, nine goddesses of the arts
and sciences in Greek mythology, were:

Calliope—epic poetry   Erato—love poetry   Thalia—comedy and pastoral poetry
Clio—history   Polyhymnia—sacred song Melpomene—tragedy
Euterpe—lyric poetry   Urania—astronomy   Terpsichore—dance

Seven Great Towns of Greece

*This English round is based on Thomas Seward's rhyme about
the great Greek poet Homer, which he wrote in 1738.
Seward's rhyme was based on a story that had circulated
since the time of the ancient Greeks.*

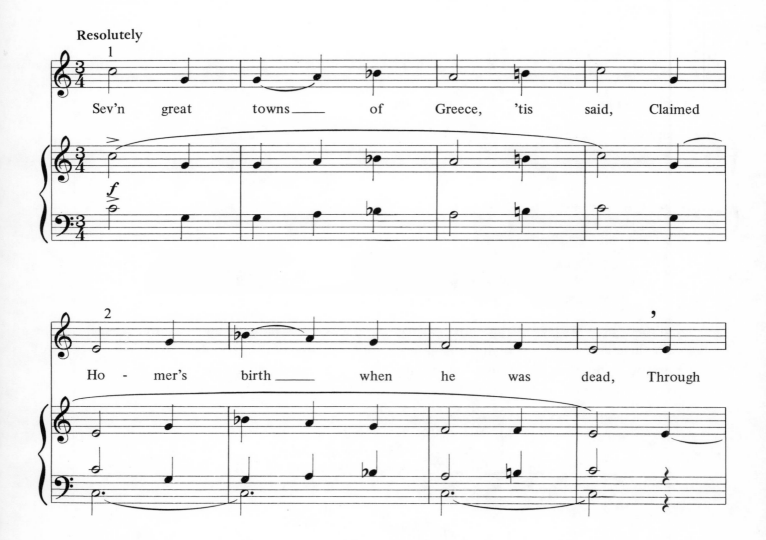

Sev'n great towns of Greece, 'tis said, Claimed
Ho - mer's birth when he was dead, Through

which,   a - live, _____   he   begged ____   his   bread.

Seven wealthy towns contend for Homer dead
Through which the living Homer begg'd his bread.

    Thomas Seward

Seven cities warr'd for Homer, being dead,
Who, living, had no roof to shroud his head.

    Thomas Heywood

[35]

Scotland's Burning

This play-party song, usually sung with appropriate motions,
was originally from England, but it is very popular in
American schools. In America the song is about Scotland burning,
but in England the words point to London's great fire.

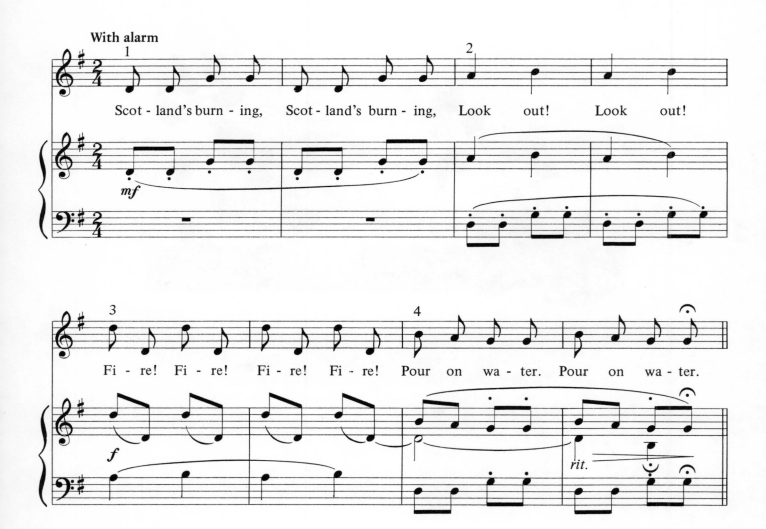

Two of the biggest fires in the world were the Great Fire of London in 1666 and the Great Chicago Fire in 1871. The London fire burned four-fifths of the city and continued for almost a week. The Chicago fire burned for only twenty-four hours but destroyed 17,450 buildings.

Scotland, as a whole, has never burned.

French Cathedrals

This French round dates back to the sixteenth century,
when it was called "Carillon de Vendôme."
In 1717 it acquired new words.
The round names four famous French cathedrals.

Or - lé - ans, Beau - gen - cy, No - tre Dam - e

de Clé - ry, Ven - dôm - e, Ven - dôm - e.

The new words, circa 1717

Quel chagrin, quel ennui,
De compter toute la nuit,
Les heures, les heures.

What a bore, what a bore,
Counting, counting all night long
The hours, the hours.

Turn Again, Whittington

*This English round was written in the mid-1400s
as "Heave and ho, Rumbelow, Row the boat,
Norman row, Row to thy leman [sweetheart]."*

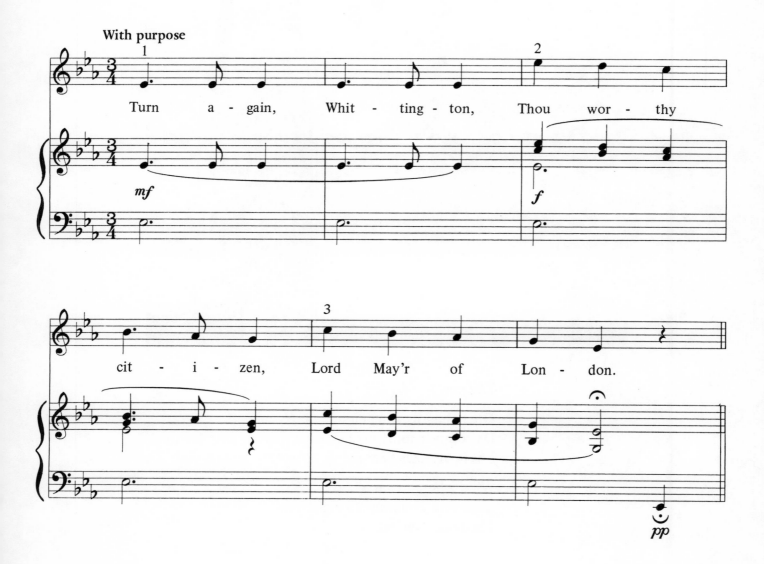

Turn a - gain, Whit - ting - ton, Thou wor - thy

cit - i - zen, Lord May'r of Lon - don.

Dick Whittington was a serving boy whose master was a famous merchant. When the master offered to carry something from each of the servants in his house to sell and try to make their fortunes, young Dick had nothing but his cat. So he sadly parted with his pet and gave it to the merchant. But without his cat, Dick had a cruel, hard time in the great house, and so he ran away. He was within hearing of the great Bow bells of London when he rested on a large stone. The bells seemed to call to him: "Turn again, Whittington, thrice Lord Mayor of London." Young Dick turned around and went back to the merchant's house. His master had returned and had sold the cat to a king whose kingdom was overrun with rats. He had a small fortune for Dick. Dick was now a very rich man. He married the merchant's daughter and became Lord Mayor of London—three times.

[41]

Frère Jacques

*One of the most famous rounds in the world, this four-part song
was originally written in old French, but it
has been translated into practically every language in the world.*

Frè - re Jac - ques, Frè - re Jac - ques, Dor - mez - vous? Dor - mez - vous?

Son - nez les ma - ti - nes, Son - nez les ma - ti - nes, Din, din, don. Din, din, don.

English:

Are you sleeping, are you sleeping,
Brother John, brother John?
Morning bells are ringing, morning bells are ringing,
Ding, ding, dong, ding, ding, dong.

Spanish:

Frey Felipe, Frey Felipe,
Duermes tu, duermes tu?
Tocan las campanas, tocan las campanas,
Tan, tan, tan, tan, tan, tan.

Yiddish:

Onkel Jakob, Onkel Jacob,
Schläfst du noch, schläfst du noch?
Ringe an der Glocke, ringe an der Glocke,
Bim, bam, bom, bim, bam, bom.

Where Is John?

A traditional American round found
throughout the Appalachian mountains.

With growing anger

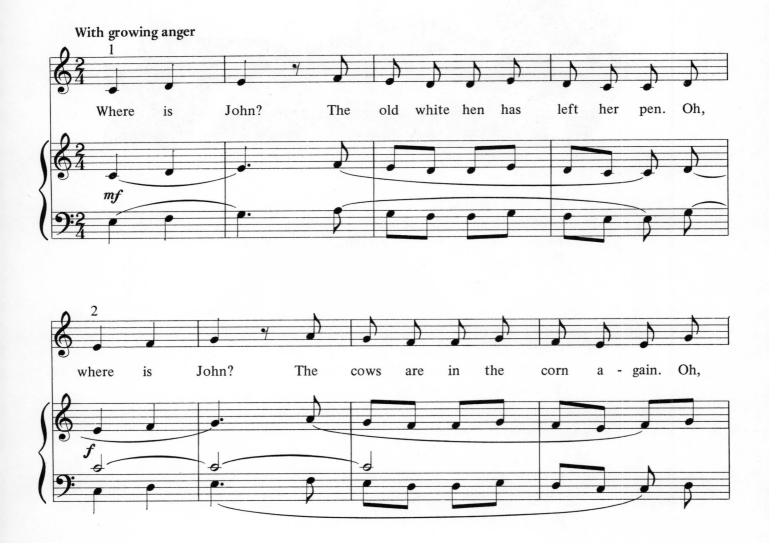

Where is John? The old white hen has left her pen. Oh,

where is John? The cows are in the corn a - gain. Oh,

Little Boy Blue, come blow your horn,
The cow's in the meadow, the sheep in the corn:
But where's the little boy who is tending the sheep?
He's under the hay-cock fast asleep.
Will you wake him? No, not I,
For if I do, he's sure to cry.

Old Nursery Rhyme, first printed in
The Pretty Songs of Tommy Thumb

[45]

The Ghost of John

This popular American round has nice ghostly effects.

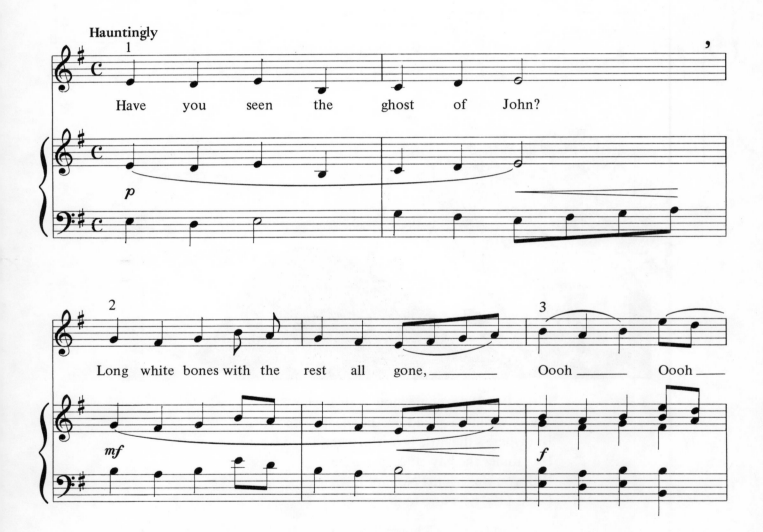

Would-n't it be chil-ly with no skin on?

Adieu! my friends, my work is done,
And to the dust I must return,
Far hence, away, my spirit flies
To find a home beyond the skies.

New England gravestone

Jack, Boy, Ho!

Pammelia, *1609, was where this four-part English round*
was first printed.

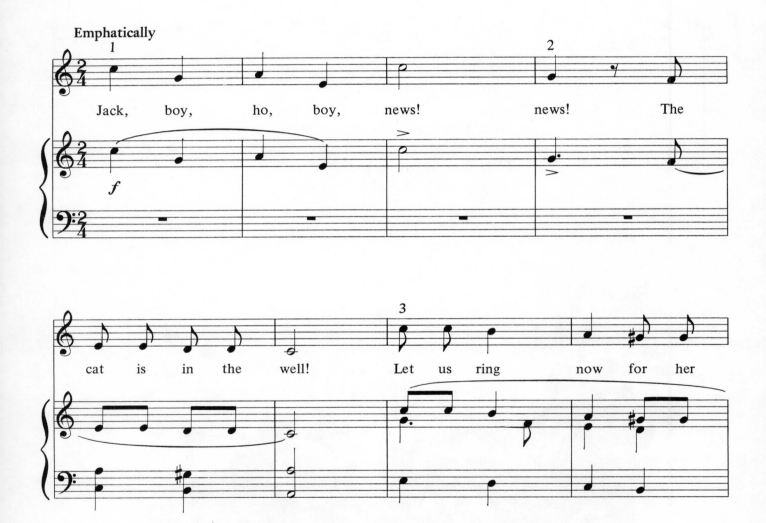

knell,　　　Ding,　dong,　　ding,　dong,　　bell.

Ding, dong bell,
Pussy's in the well.
Who put her in?
Little Johnny Green.
Who pulled her out?
Little Tommy Stout.

Nursery rhyme
printed mid-1700s

*This can be sung in six parts as well, the voices entering
after two measures, instead of three. It's more difficult,
but it provides a constant "Jack, boy, ho, boy," which is
fun; and it alters the harmonies in an interesting way.*

Jane Glover

*A four-part round from England,
this song is sometimes known as
Joan Glover, for in early England
the two names—Jane and Joan—were
often interchangeable. The round was
first printed in* Deuteromelia, *1609.*

Jane, Joan, Jenny, and Jean
Went bird's nesting on the green,
They found a bird's nest with five eggs in,
They each took one, and left four behind.
        How?

The answer is that since
Jane, Joan, Jenny, and Jean are
all the same name, or nicknames,
only one girl went on the field trip.

My Dame Hath

This tongue twister is a four-part English round
written by Matthew White about 1630.

MATTHEW WHITE

Liltingly, but be careful not to trip

My Dame hath a lame tame crane. My Dame hath a crane that is lame. Pray,

gen - tle Jane, take my crane that is lame, And go home a - gain.

Here is another tongue-tangler:

> The Leith police dismisseth us,
> I'm thankful sir, to say;
> The Leith police dismisseth us,
> They thought we sought to stay.
> The Leith police dismisseth us,
> We both sighed sighs apiece,
> And the sigh that we sighed as we said good-bye
> Was the size of the Leith police.

Sandy McNab

A delightful three-part Scottish round, this was written
in the nineteenth century by an unknown composer.

There was an old fel - low named San - dy Mc - Nab, Who

had for his sup - per a ver - y fine crab, And

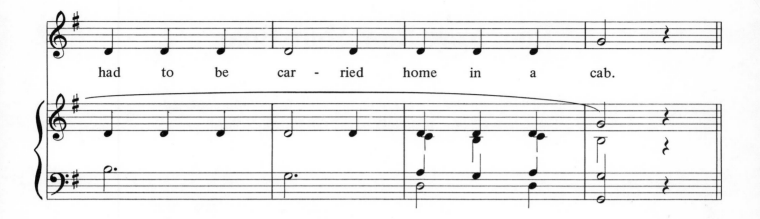

had to be car - ried home in a cab.

He who eats on a full stomach
digs his grave with his teeth.

Russian proverb

Today feasting, tomorrow
reclining in the coffin.

French proverb

He who eats only one dish
rarely needs the physician.

English proverb

Row, Row, Row Your Boat

*One of the most popular of the nursery rounds, this simple song is a
four-part American round, probably written in the nineteenth century.*

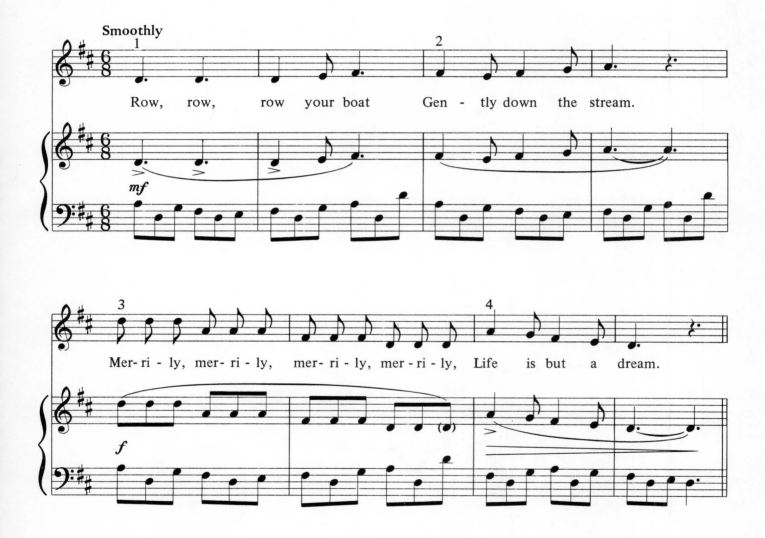

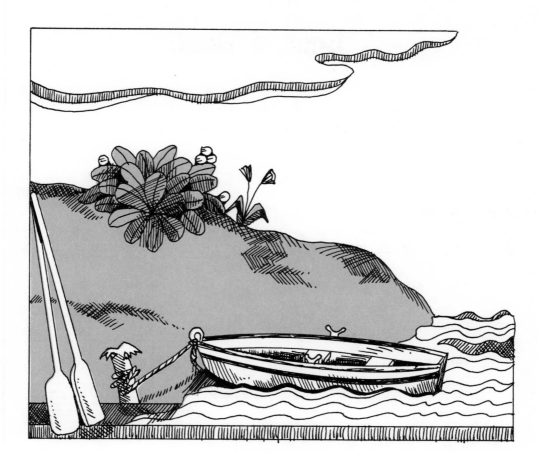

The sailors say:

If the cat washes her face over the ear,
'Tis a sign the weather'll be fine and clear.

When seabirds fly to land,
A storm is at hand.

Red sky in the morning, sailors take warning.
Red sky at night, sailors' delight.

[57]

A Boat, a Boat!

*John Jenkins, an Englishman who lived from
1592 to 1678, wrote this three-part round.*

JOHN JENKINS

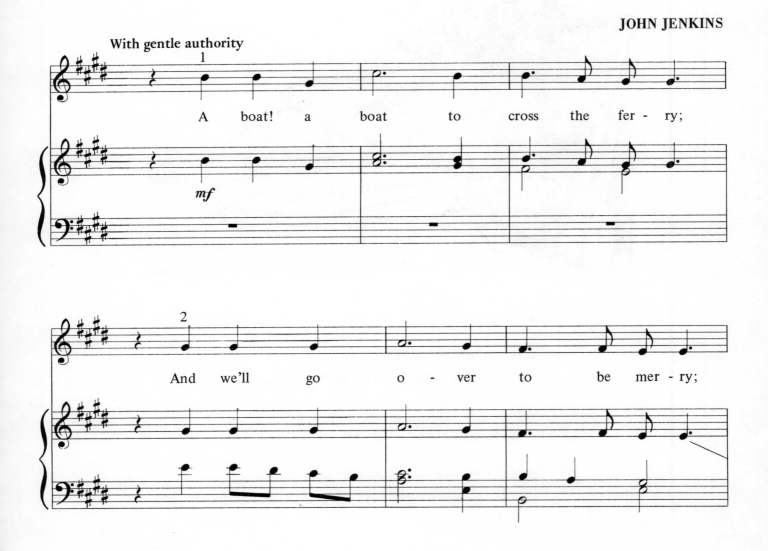

And while ___ we ___ float sing hey down der - ry.

Bring out L.H.

A chieftain to the Highlands bound
Cries, "Boatman, do not tarry!
And I'll give thee a silver pound
To row us o'er the ferry."

Thomas Campbell,
"Lord Ullin's Daughter"

Canoe Round

Here is a four-part round
written in 1918 by
Margaret Embers McGee.

MARGARET EMBERS McGEE

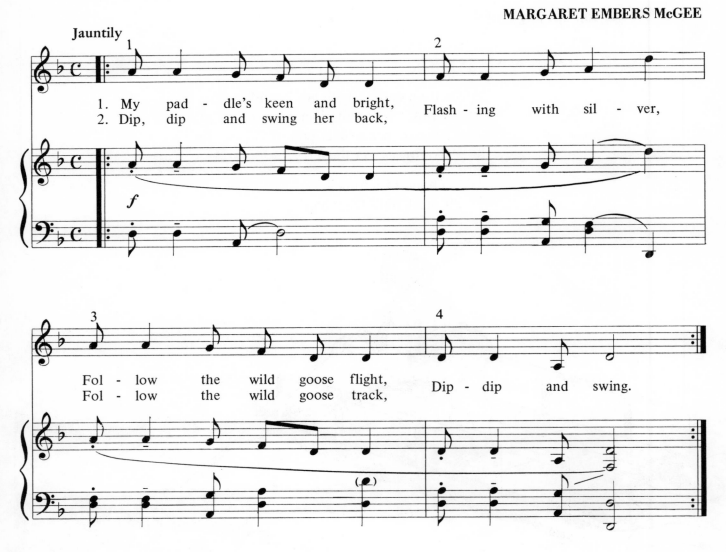

1. My pad - dle's keen and bright, Flash - ing with sil - ver,
2. Dip, dip and swing her back,

Fol - low the wild goose flight, Dip - dip and swing.
Fol - low the wild goose track,

Oh, for a capful of wind!

Sailor's prayer

Where Are You Going?

Henry Purcell, the English composer who lived from 1659 to 1695
and wrote the first important English opera,
wrote this simple four-part round, based on an old nursery rhyme.

HENRY PURCELL

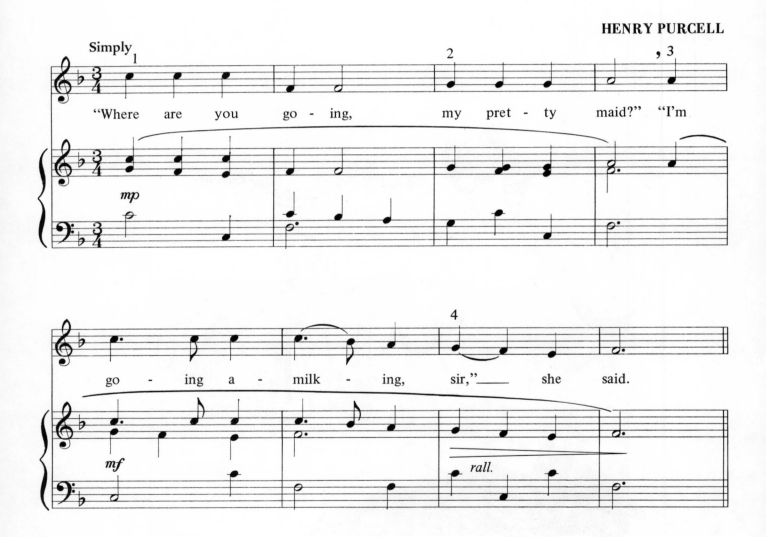

"Where are you go-ing, my pret-ty maid?" "I'm

go-ing a-milk-ing, sir,"___ she said.

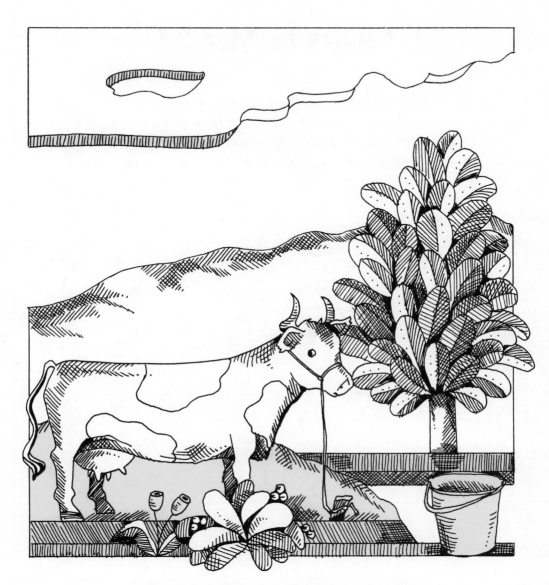

Milkman, milkman, where have you been?
In buttermilk channel up to my chin.
I spilt my milk and I spoilt my clothes,
And got a long icicle hung to my nose.

Nineteenth-century rhyme

[63]

Chairs to Mend: I

Sellers in the streets of Europe and America used to sing out their wares. It was one of the earliest forms of advertisement. There are many rounds, such as this three-part English round, that are based on such street cries.

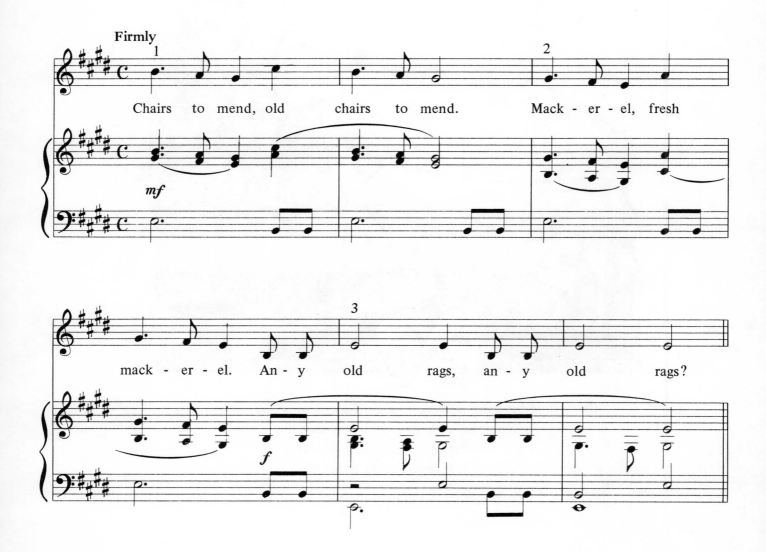

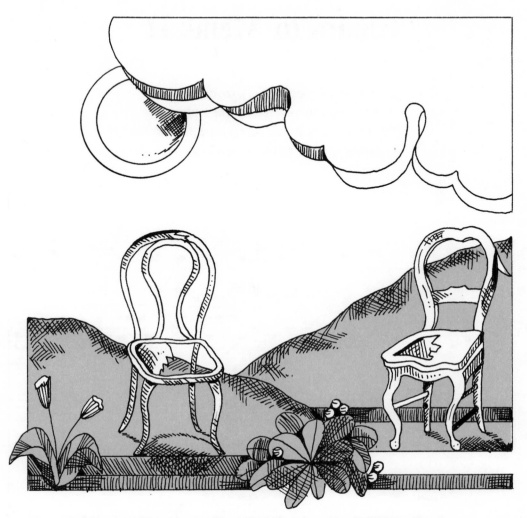

Orlando Gibbons, 1583–1625, was an English composer
of famous songs called "London Street Cries":

God give you good morrow my masters, past three
a-clocke and a faire morning. New mussels, new
lily-white mussels. Hot codlings hot. New cocles,
new great cocles. New greate sprats, new lamprils.
New fresh herrings. New haddocks new. New thorn-
backs new. Hot apple pies hot. Hot pippin pies hot. . . .

Chairs to Mend: II

Philip Hayes was a professor at
Oxford University in the 1700s.
He composed this three-part round
based on the London street cries.

PHILIP HAYES

mack - er - el, new mack - er - el. Old rags, an - y old rags, Take

mon - ey for your old rags. An - y hare - skins or rab - bit skins?

. . . Buy any ink, will you buy any ink? Ha'ye any rats or mice to kill?

[67]

White Sand and Gray Sand

*A traditional English round, this is based
on an eighteenth-century street cry.*

White sand and gray sand; Who'll buy my white sand? Who'll buy my gray sand?

. . . Fine pomegranates fine. Ha'ye any old bellowes or trayes to mend?

Cherries So Ripe

Here is yet another English street cry made into a four-part round.

Informatively

1. Cher-ries so ripe and so round, The best in the mar-ket ___ found.
2.
3. On - ly a pen-ny a pound. Who will buy?
4.

mf

f

p

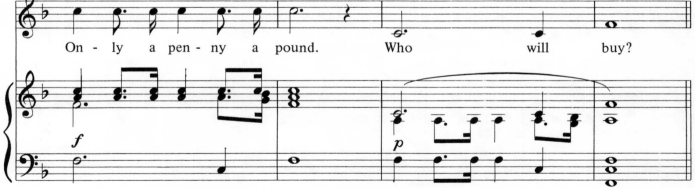

. . . Will ye buy any milke or frumenty? Ha' you work for a Tinker?

[69]

Buy My Dainty Fine Beans

*An early-nineteenth-century market cry
that was made into a three-part round.*

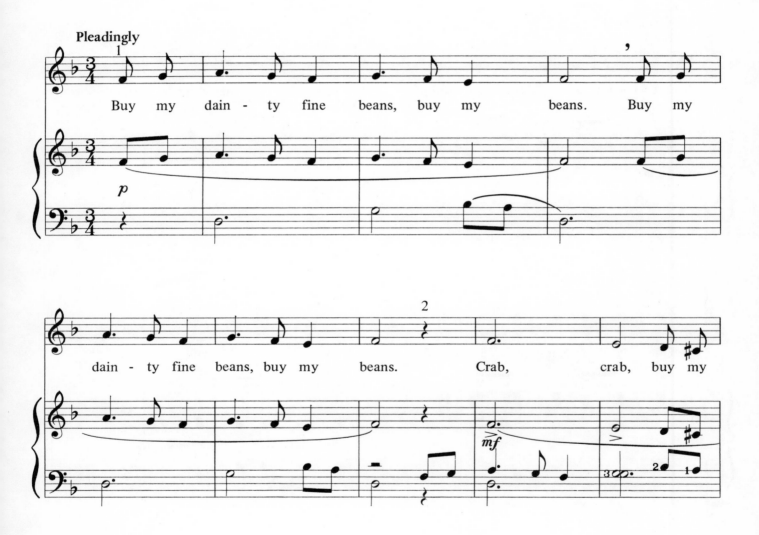

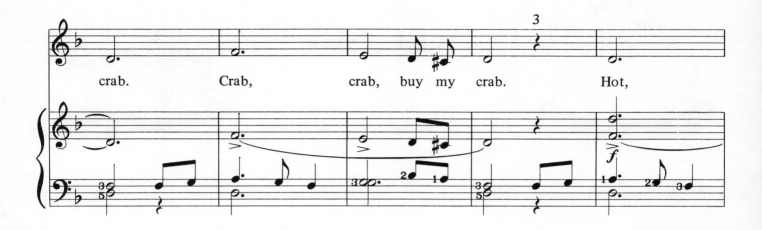

crab.   Crab,   crab,   buy my   crab.   Hot,

hot mut - ton pies.   Hot,   hot mut - ton pies.

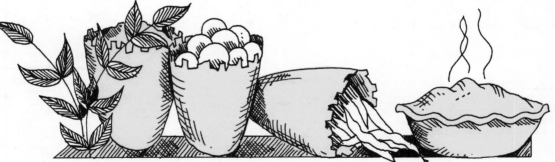

. . . Swepe chimney swepe Mistris, with a hey dery, dery, dery, swepe.

Soul Cakes

*This traditional English round is
probably from the seventeenth century.*

Pleadingly

Soul, soul, soul cake, Please, good Ma - ma, a soul cake. An

ap - ple, a plum, a peach, or a cher - ry, An - y good thing to ___

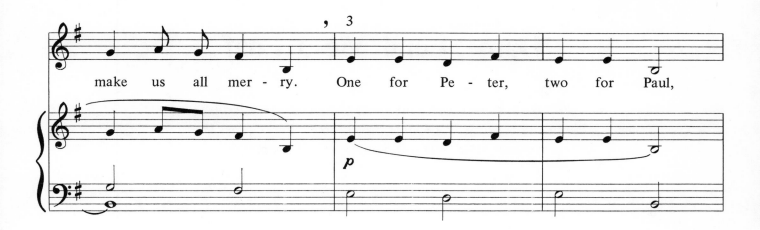

make us all mer - ry. One for Pe - ter, two for Paul,

Three for Him who made us ___ all. ___

In Russia soul cakes were gingerbread and sweet tarts.
In Austria soul cakes were left on the graves for the
     hungry dead.
In England soul cakes were cooked on October 28 and
     eaten on Halloween, All Souls' Day.
In Wales the soul cakes were distributed to the poor.
In ancient Egypt soul cakes were left inside the tombs.
In old China soul cakes were baked for the Festival
     of the Hungry Ghosts.
In India soul cakes were honied rice balls.

Dame, Lend Me a Loaf

This British three-part round was first put down in print in Pammelia in 1609 by Thomas Ravenscroft. Three years later, it was printed in David Melvill's 1612 collection.

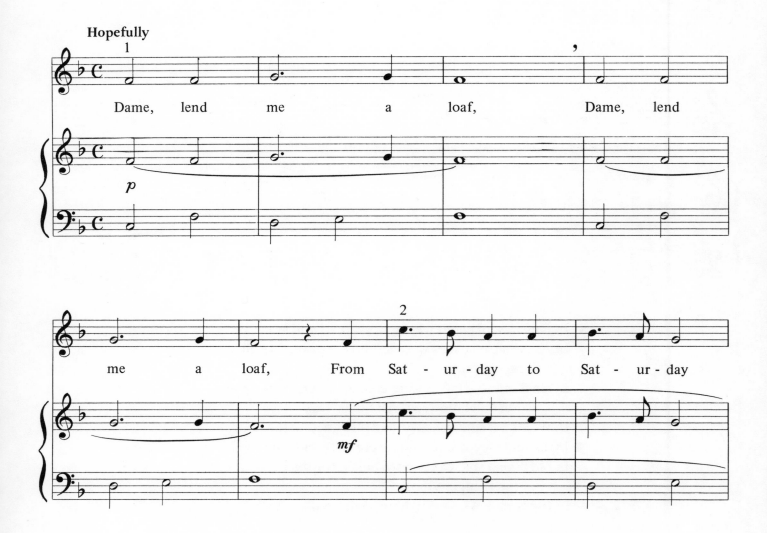

And lon - ger if you lon - ger may.   Dame, lend

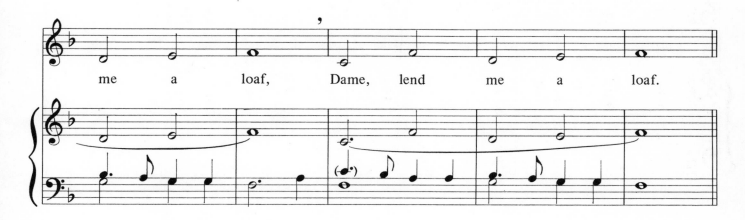

me a loaf,   Dame, lend   me a   loaf.

Dame, get up and bake your pies,
Bake your pies, bake your pies,
Dame, get up and bake your pies
On Christmas day in the morning.

Eighteenth-century song

Christmas Is Coming

This old song was first published as a nursery rhyme
in the seventeenth century in England.
The round was written by F. Nesbitt for three parts.

F. NESBITT

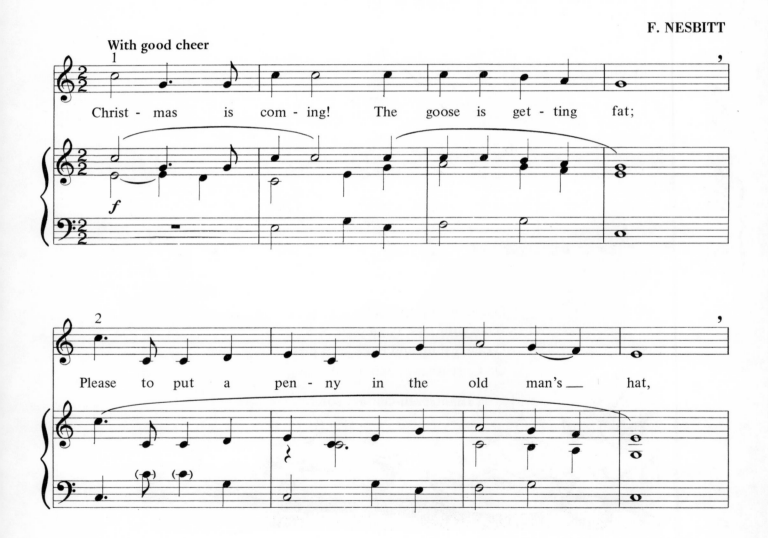

Christ - mas is com - ing! The goose is get - ting fat;

Please to put a pen - ny in the old man's ___ hat,

3

Please   to put   a   pen - ny   in the   old   man's   hat.

Christmas is coming, the geese are getting fat,
Please to put a penny in an old man's hat;
If you haven't a penny, a ha'penny will do,
If you haven't got a ha'penny, God bless you.

The original nursery rhyme

[77]

Come Follow, Follow

John Hilton, an English composer, lived from 1599 to 1657.
He composed this three-part round, little suspecting that it would become
popular in American and British schools three centuries later.

JOHN HILTON

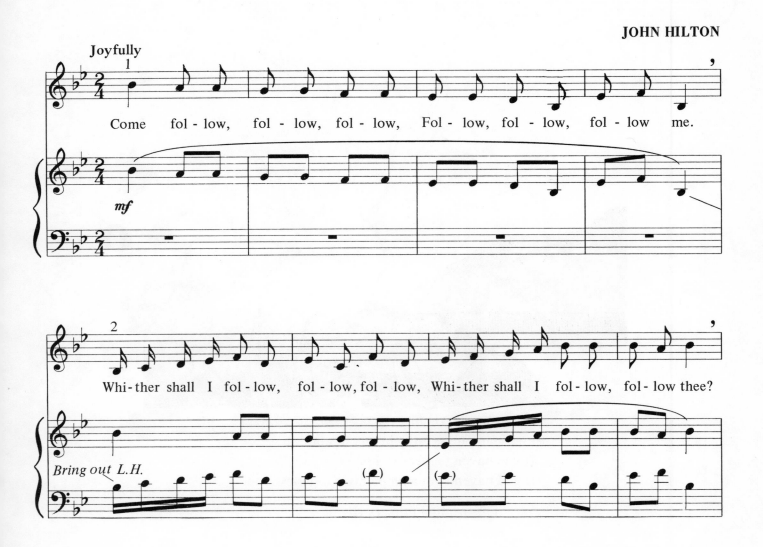

Come fol - low, fol - low, fol - low, Fol - low, fol - low, fol - low me.

Whi - ther shall I fol - low, fol - low, fol - low, Whi - ther shall I fol - low, fol - low thee?

To the green-wood, to the green-wood, To the green-wood, green-wood tree.

Under the greenwood tree
Who loves to lie with me,
And turn his merry note
Unto the sweet bird's throat,
Come hither, come hither, come hither:
Here shall he see
No enemy
But winter and rough weather.

Shakespeare, *As You Like It*

Summer Is A-Coming In

A monk who lived in the thirteenth century in Reading Abbey,
John of Fornsete, wrote this song. The word "verteth" means
"seeks the green meadow." The original spelling of the title was
"Sumer Is Icumen In" and is often printed that way in songbooks.

JOHN of FORNSETE

Sing cuck - oo.   Ewe now bleat - eth af - ter lamb, low'th

Midsummer Eve in England used to be celebrated with the baking of a "dumb cake" made by two girls, who did not speak to one another. They each took half the cake to hide under their pillows. The man each dreamed of would be the man she would marry.

Two make it.
Two bake it.
Two break it.

All Is Silent

This traditional three-part German round
is translated by David Stemple.

All is si - lent; Night - in - gales beck - on
Al - les schwei - get; Nach - ti - gal - len

With their sweet me - lo - dies, With their sweet me - lo - dies,
Lock - en mit süs - sen Me - lo - di - en

[84]

Riddles from *The Girl's Own Book,* 1837

What bird is what we do at dinner?
What bird is disliked by mice?
What bird is like a warm country?
What bird is what wicked men are doing?
What bird is an instrument to raise weights?
What bird do leaves grow on?

Answers

Swallow
Cat-bird
Turkey
Robin (robbing)
Crane
Stork (stalk)

Kookaburra

The Girl Scouts of America introduced this
Australian round to America. British Girl Guides
sing it, too. It is by Marion Sinclair.

MARION SINCLAIR

Kook - a - bur - ra sits on the old gum tree, ____

1. Mer - ry, mer - ry king of the bush is he. ____ Laugh, Kook-a-bur - ra,
2. Eat - ing all the gum drops he can see. ____ Stop, Kook-a-bur - ra,

Laugh, Kook - a - bur - ra,   Gay your life must be.
Stop,   Save some life there for me.

The kookaburra, or laughing jackass, is a bird of the kingfisher family. It lives in Australia and is noted for its peculiar cry.

Thou Poor Bird

This sad, soaring little round is from England;
the author and composer are unknown.

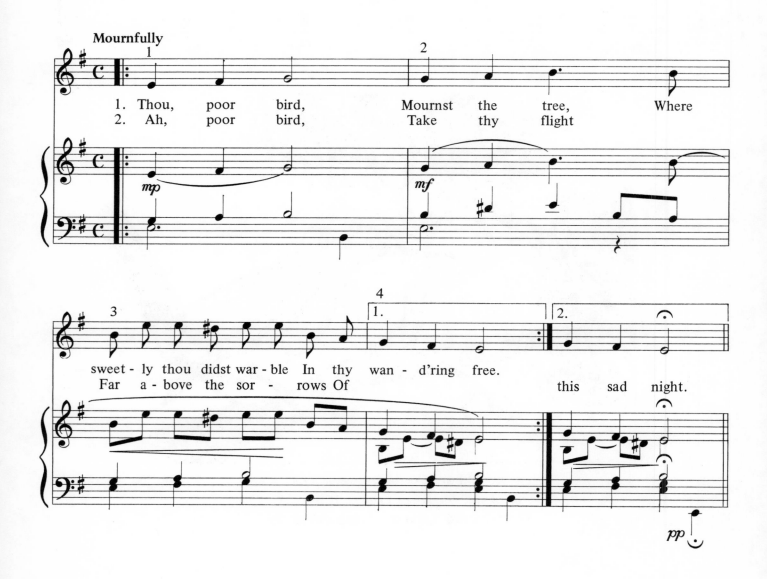

1. Thou, poor bird, Mournst the tree, Where sweet-ly thou didst war-ble In thy wan-d'ring free.
2. Ah, poor bird, Take thy flight Far a-bove the sor-rows Of this sad night.

Three hundred years ago in Peking, an unknown genius made a strange musical pipe that could be attached to the base of a bird's tail feathers. Soon the skies above Peking were filled with melody as doves, fitted with the flutes, flew high over the city streets.

Try singing this simultaneously with "Hey Ho, Nobody's Home" or in canon with "Rose, Rose" ("Rose, Rose" entering on the second measure).

Why Shouldn't My Goose

*From England comes this anonymous
four-part round that is several centuries old.*

Indignantly (with excellent diction)

Why should-n't my goose   Sing as well as thy goose

When I paid for my goose   Twice as much as thou?

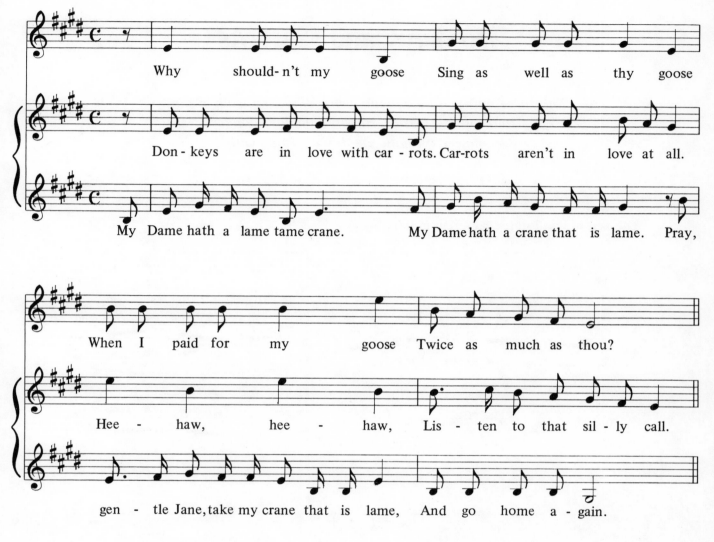

Why should-n't my goose Sing as well as thy goose

Don - keys are in love with car - rots. Car-rots aren't in love at all.

My Dame hath a lame tame crane. My Dame hath a crane that is lame. Pray,

When I paid for my goose Twice as much as thou?

Hee - haw, hee - haw, Lis - ten to that sil - ly call.

gen - tle Jane, take my crane that is lame, And go home a - gain.

Try singing this with the songs from pages 52 and 92.

Donkeys and Carrots

This silly round is from Belgium, where the song really means:
"Donkeys love carrots, carrots don't love donkeys.
Hee-haw, it is idiotic, but it is charming also."

This is a very sad song—keep that in mind.

Don - keys are in love with car - rots. Car - rots aren't in love at all.
Les ân - es aim' les car - rot - tes. Les car - rott' n'aim'pas les ân's.

Hee - haw, hee - haw, Lis - ten to that sil - ly call.
Hee - haw, hee - haw, C'est i - diot mais c'est mar - rant.

The Chinese immortal Chang Kuo-lao was a magician of the highest
rank. Whenever he stopped for the night, he would dismount
from his mule, fold it up like paper, and put the animal into his cap.

Sweetly Sings the Donkey

An anonymous three-part round from England,
this song is popular with camp and school groups.

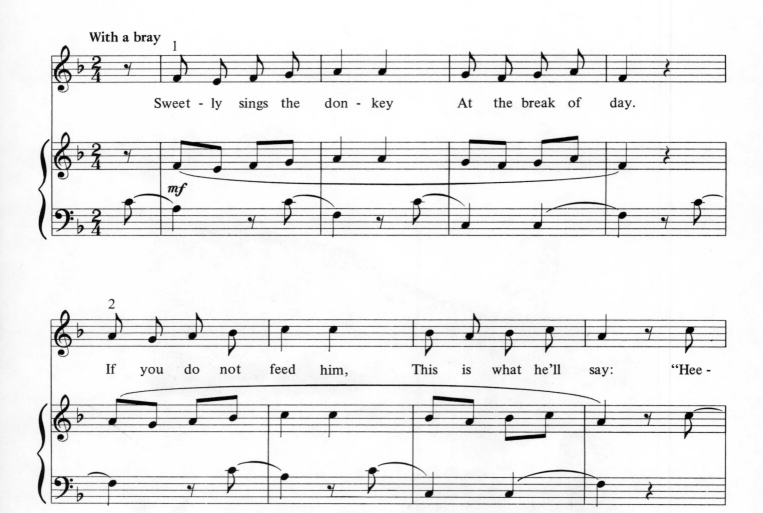

Sweet - ly sings the don - key At the break of day.

If you do not feed him, This is what he'll say: "Hee -

haw,   hee - haw,   hee - haw, hee - haw, hee - haw."

Donkey, donkey, do not bray,
Mend your pace and trot away;
Indeed, the market's almost done,
My butter's melting in the sun.

    Early nursery rhyme

[95]

Hey Ho, to the Greenwood

David Melvill published this song in his book of rounds, 1612.
The words were written by an anonymous author,
the music attributed to the composer William Byrd (1540–1623).

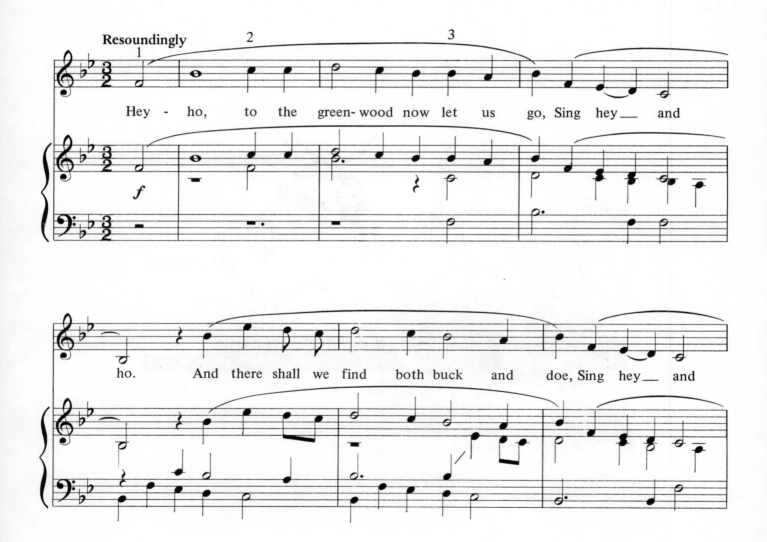

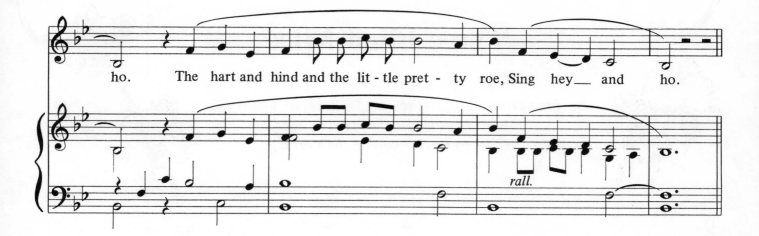

ho. The hart and hind and the lit - tle pret - ty roe, Sing hey__ and ho.

My heart's in the Highlands, my heart is not
    here;
My heart's in the Highlands a-chasing the
    deer;
Chasing the wild deer, and following the
    roe—
My heart's in the Highlands, wherever I go.

    Robert Burns,
    "My Heart's in the Highlands"

Three Blind Mice

First printed in Ravenscroft's Deuteromelia *in 1609, this grisly little round has been called the "best-known round in the world."*

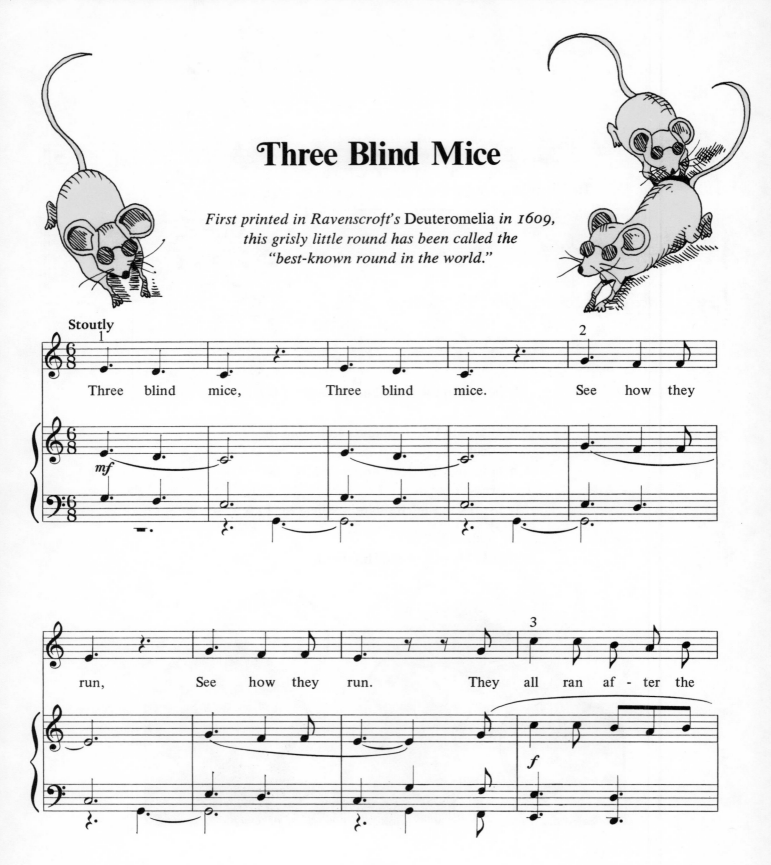

Three blind mice, Three blind mice. See how they run, See how they run. They all ran af - ter the

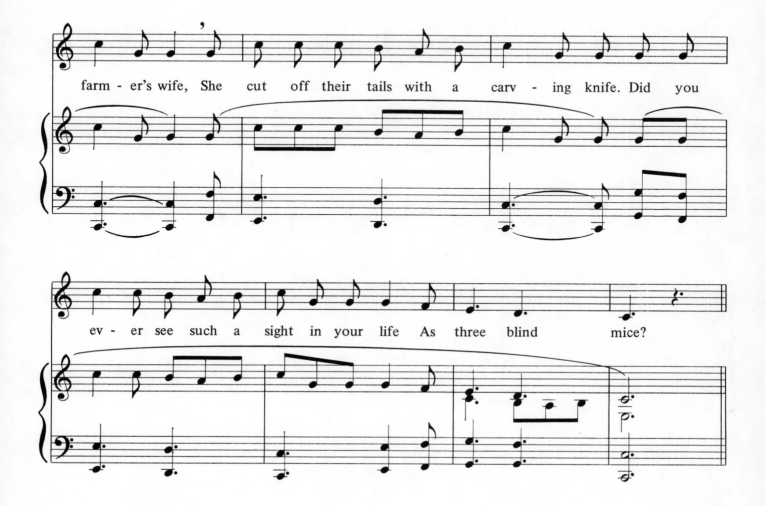

farm - er's wife, She cut off their tails with a carv - ing knife. Did you

ev - er see such a sight in your life As three blind mice?

Field mice were sentenced to leave the countryside around Stelvio, North Italy within two weeks, according to court records dated May 2, 1520.

The mice were charged with having gravely damaged the crops and despite a spirited defense, were found guilty and ordered out. Old and infirm mice as well as the young were allowed a month to pack up and go, the record showed.

At the same time, the record of the trial found in the Archives of the Court of Glorenza in Val Venosta near Bolzano, showed that the farmers of Stelvio had to build bridges for the mice over the streams in the area.   *The New York Times*

[99]

The Frogs

This American round has four parts.

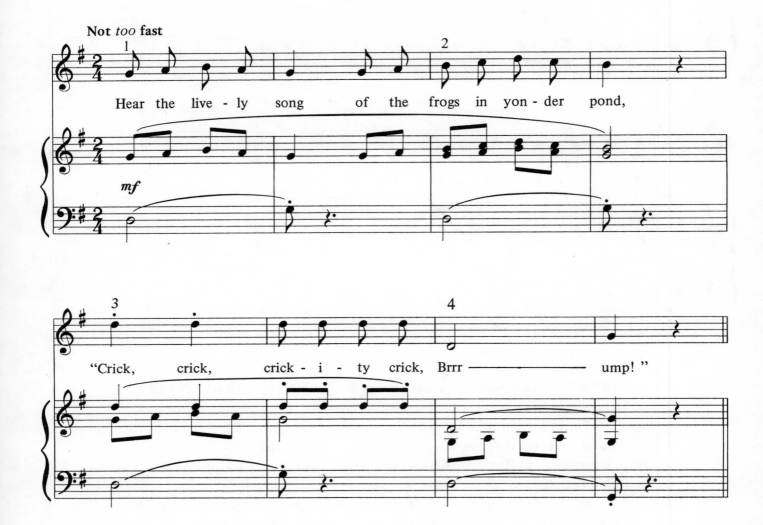

"Oh, father," said a little frog sitting one day by the pool. "I have seen a terrible monster. It was big as a mountain, with horns on its head, a long tail and hoofs divided in two."

"Tush, child," said the old frog. "That was only the farmer's ox. It isn't so big, only a bit taller than I."

"Oh he was much bigger than you, father," said the little frog.

So the old one blew himself out and out and out. "As big as that?" he said.

"Much bigger yet."

Again the old one blew himself out.

"Bigger, father, bigger."

So the old frog took a mighty breath and blew and blew and swelled and swelled. And then he said, "I am sure the ox is not as big as . . ." But at that moment he burst.

Moral: Self-conceit may lead to self-destruction.

A fable from Aesop

The Sun It Rises

*Thomas Tallis wrote the original music from which this round
was created. Tallis lived in the sixteenth century and was
a prominent English composer who was known as "the Father
of English Church Music." He wrote songs with many parts.
One of them was said to have had forty parts, surely a record.
Harvey Spevak wrote the lyrics for this version.*

THOMAS TALLIS

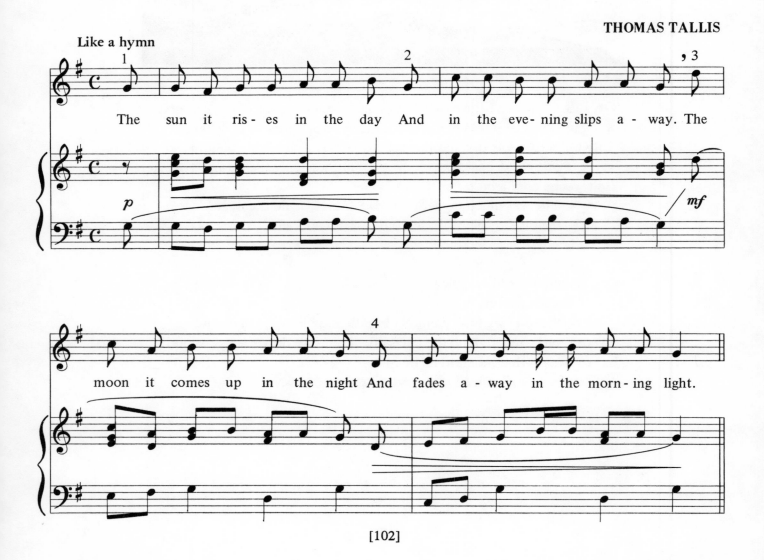

Like a hymn

The sun it ris - es in the day And in the eve - ning slips a - way. The

moon it comes up in the night And fades a - way in the morn - ing light.

The sun was shining on the sea,
　　Shining with all his might.
He did his very best to make
　　The billows smooth and bright—
And this was odd, because it was
　　The middle of the night.

from "The Walrus and the Carpenter"
in *Through the Looking-Glass*
by Lewis Carroll

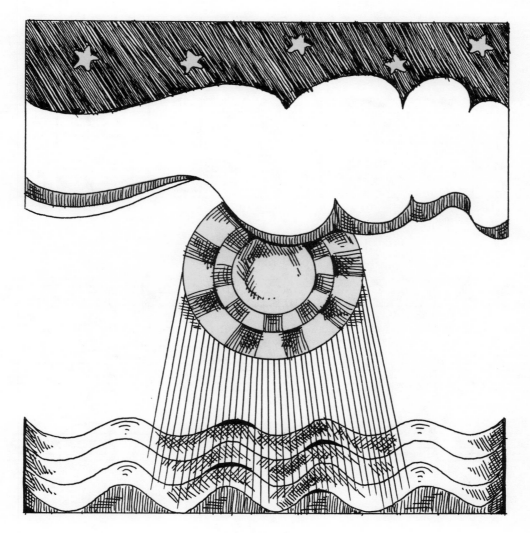

Ho! Ev'ry Sleeper Waken

This three-part round is English,
probably nineteenth-century.

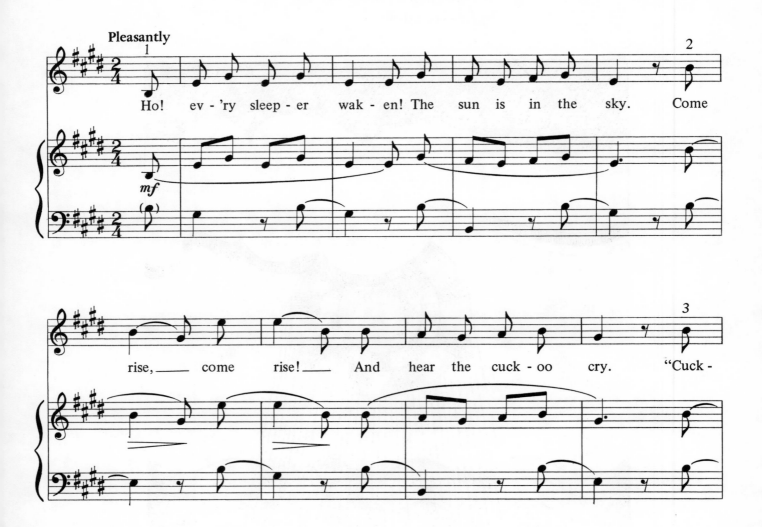

Pleasantly

Ho! ev - 'ry sleep - er wak - en! The sun is in the sky. Come

rise,___ come rise!___ And hear the cuck - oo cry. "Cuck -

oo!   Cuck - oo!   Wake up!   Be spry! "

Wake up, Jacob,
Day's a-breakin',
Peas in the pot and hoecakes bakin'.
Bacon's in the pan and coffee's in the pot,
Come on round and get it while it's hot.
WAKE SNAKES AND BITE A BISCUIT!

American cowboy getting-up holler

Goodnight to You All

An anonymous three-part English round.

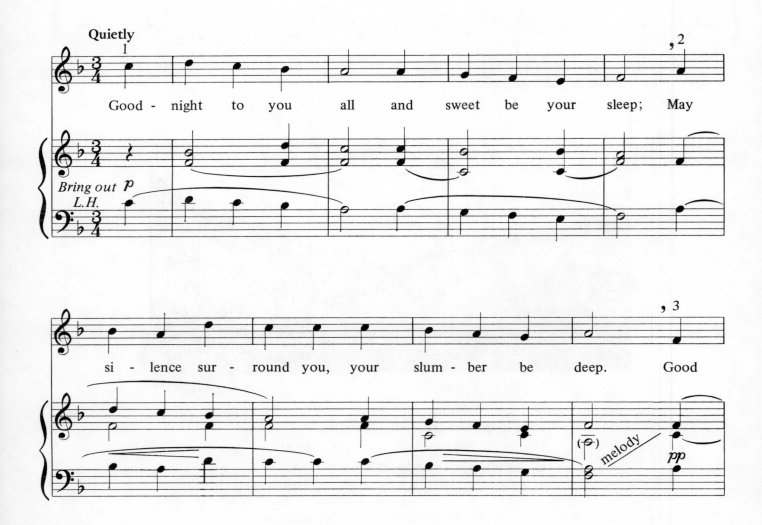

Good - night to you all and sweet be your sleep; May
si - lence sur - round you, your slum - ber be deep. Good

Oh, slowly, slowly run the horses of the night.

Ovid

Shaker Life

*The Shakers are an unusual religious group who were founded
by Mother Ann Lee in the 1770s. Mother Ann was an English-
woman who, with eight of her followers, went to America where
her Shaker communities flourished. This round is based on the
Shaker dance song "Come life, Shaker life," composed by Elder
Issachar Bates of the Mount Lebanon Shaker community in 1835.*

ELDER ISSACHAR BATES

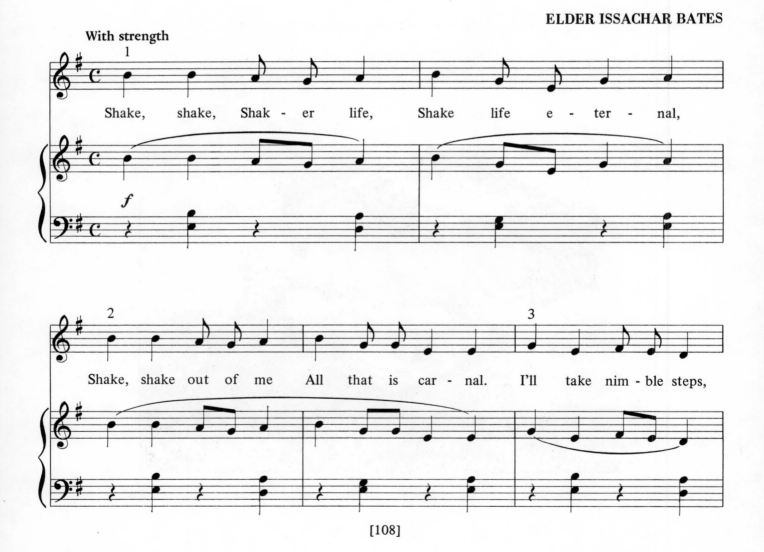

With strength

Shake, shake, Shak - er life, Shake life e - ter - nal,

Shake, shake out of me All that is car - nal. I'll take nim - ble steps,

I'll be a Da - vid, I'll show Mi - chael twice How he be - hav - ed.

Work as though you would live a thousand years,
Work as though you would die tomorrow.

Shaker saying

Shalom Chaverim

This Hebrew round is known throughout the world.
It is pronounced: "Shah-loam hah-ver-reem, lay-heet-rah-oat" and
means "Good-bye, friends, until we meet again, good-bye, peace."
It can say all that because the word "Shalom" means
"hello" and "good-bye" and "peace"—a most fortunate word.

Fare thee well for I must leave thee,
Do not let this parting grieve thee.

Old song: "There Is a Tavern in the Town"

*This can be sung in the eight parts, creating
blocks of repeated sound. Why not experiment
with it? Start with fewer parts, entering at two-
measure intervals; add more; take away some.
Have fun!*

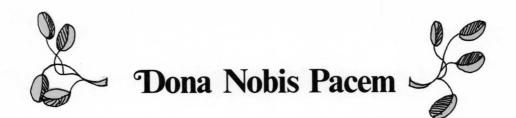

Dona Nobis Pacem

*"Grant us peace" say the words of this Latin three-part round,
which is usually attributed to the sixteenth-century composer
of polyphonic (many-voiced) church music, Giovanni Palestrina.
Palestrina, who composed over 950 pieces of music, lived 1526–1594.*

GIOVANNI PALESTRINA

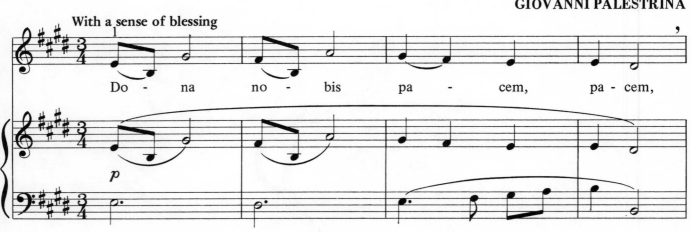

Do - na no - bis pa - cem, pa - cem,

Do - na — no - bis pa - cem. Do -

[112]

na no - bis pa - cem, Do - na no - bis

pa - cem. Do - na no - bis

pa - cem, Do - na no - bis pa - cem.

Rounds About Rounds

This round was written especially for the book.
It has proved to the authors that singing and
playing rounds is fun—and writing them is hard work.

BARBARA GREEN and JANE YOLEN

on to the end. You'll make bet - ter mu - sic when you have a friend, go - ing

you have a friend, go - ing Rounds a - bout rounds a - bout rounds a - bout rounds.

Sources of Rounds

FB—*The Fireside Book of Children's Songs,* by Marie Winn (New York: Simon & Schuster, 1965).

GB—*The Gambit Book of Children's Songs,* by Donald Mitchell and Roderick Bliss (Boston: Gambit, 1970).

AEL—*An Anthology of Elizabethan Lute Songs, Madrigals, and Rounds,* by Noah Greenberg (New York: Norton, 1955).

ST—*Sing Together: A Girl Scout Handbook* (Girl Scouts of America, 1949).

BB—*A Book of Ballads, Songs, and Snatches,* by Haig and Regina Shekerjian (New York: Harper & Row, 1965).

FSB—*The Fireside Song Book of Birds and Beasts,* by Jane Yolen and Barbara Green (New York: Simon & Schuster, 1972).

EM—*Exploring Music: Teacher's Edition,* by Eunice Boardman and Beth Landis (New York: Holt, Rinehart and Winston, 1966).

RR—*Rounds and Rounds,* by Mary C. Taylor (New York: William Sloane Associates, 1946).

SGG—*Songs for Girl Guides* (Girl Guide Association).

GSSB—*Girl Scout Song Book* (1925, 1929).

RRWG—*Rounds and Rounds We Go,* by Mary C. Taylor (Brooklyn: Penfor Music Publications, 1969).

WM—*The Word of Mouth Round Book,* by the Word of Mouth Chorus (Plainfield, Vt., 1973).

101—*101 Rounds for Singing,* World Around Songs (Delaware, Ohio: Informal Music Service).

All Things Must Perish—101.

Oh, Music, Sweet Music—RR, RRWG.

Now We'll Make the Rafters Ring—RR.

Make New Friends—EM, 101.

Merrily, Merrily—ST.

Viva la Musica—ST.

The Bell Doth Toll—ST (The Bell), EM, 101.

White Coral Bells—EM.

Little Bells of Westminster—ST (The Little Bells), EM.

Great Tom Is Cast—GB, ST, RR.

Oh, How Lovely Is the Evening—FB, ST (Lovely Evening), EM (Lovely Evening), 101 (Lovely Evening).

Rose, Rose—101.

Early to Bed—ST, SGG.

Man's Life's a Vapor—GSSB, 101.

Hey Ho, Nobody's Home—ST, RR, 101.

The Wise Men Were but Seven—RRWG.

Seven Great Towns of Greece—RR, GSSB (Seven Great Towns).

Scotland's Burning—FB.

French Cathedrals—ST, BB, EM, 101.

Turn Again, Whittington—GB, RR.

Frère Jacques—FB, GB, RR, 101.

Where Is John?—EM, 101.

The Ghost of John—FB (Have You Seen the Ghost of John).

Jack, Boy, Ho!—ST, RR.

Jane Glover—ST, RR, RRWG, 101.

My Dame Hath—GB (My Dame Hath a Lame Tame Crane), ST (The Lame Crane), FSB (My Dame Hath a Lame, Tame Crane), SSG (My Dame Hath a Lame Tame Crane).

Sandy McNab—RR, RRWG.

Row, Row, Row Your Boat—FB, RR, 101.

A Boat, a Boat!—RR, SGG.

Canoe Round—101.

Where Are You Going?—RRWG.

Chairs to Mend: I—ST, RRWG, 101.

Chairs to Mend: II—RR.

White Sand and Gray Sand—ST, RR, WM, 101.

Cherries So Ripe—EM, 101.

Buy My Dainty Fine Beans—ST (Dainty Fine Beans), RR.

Soul Cakes—WM.

Dame, Lend Me a Loaf—RR, RRWG.

Christmas Is Coming—SGG.

Come Follow, Follow—ST, RR (Come Follow to the Greenwood Tree), SGG, 101.

Summer Is A-Coming In—GB, ST, RR, WM, 101.

All Is Silent—ST, 101.

Kookaburra—FB, GB, 101.

Thou Poor Bird—FSB, GSSB, 101.

Why Shouldn't My Goose—FB, GB (My Goose), FSB, EM.

Donkeys and Carrots—101.

Sweetly Sings the Donkey—GB, FSB.

Hey Ho, to the Greenwood—GB, AEL, FSB, RR.

Three Blind Mice—FSB.

The Frogs—ST (Frog Round), 101.

The Sun It Rises—WM.

Ho! Ev'ry Sleeper Waken—Known to the arranger.

Goodnight to You All—RRWG (Good Night), 101.

Shaker Life—WM.

Shalom Chaverim—101.

Dona Nobis Pacem—GB, RR, WM.

Rounds About Rounds—(original).

Sources of Additional Material

DQ—*Dictionary of Quotations*, by Bergen Evans, (New York: Delacorte Press, 1968).

AMG—*Annotated Mother Goose*, by William S. Baring-Gould and Cecil Baring-Gould, (New York: Bramhall House, 1962).

RO—*Ring Out! A Book of Bells,* by Jane Yolen, (New York: Seabury, 1974).

AP—*African Proverbs,* by Charlotte & Wolff Leslau, (Mount Vernon, N.Y.: Peter Pauper Press, 1962).

"Since singing": from William Byrd's *Songs of Sadness*, 1588.

"James Green": from Francis W. Galpin, *Old English Instruments of Music*, cited in *Ballads, Songs and Snatches*, by Haig & Regina Shekerjian (New York: Harper & Row, 1965).

"Sing, sing": AMG.

"He is no friend": cited in 1976 calendar produced by the Society of Friends.

"Tom he was": AMG.

"Music hath": DQ.

"To call the fold": RO.

"Little Dawn Bird": cited in *What's in the Names of Flowers*, by Peter Limburg (New York: Coward McCann, 1974).

"A fool": DQ.

"The most famous clock tune": RO.

"I am the voice of life": RO.

"Early to bed": first quotation found in DQ; second frequently on the lips of the author's father!

"I am a maid": old song known to author.

"The muses": cited in *The World Book Encyclopedia*.

"Seven wealthy towns": both in DQ.

"Two of the biggest fires": cited in *The World Book Encyclopedia*.

"Quel chagrin": cited in *Ballads, Songs and Snatches*.

"Dick Whittington": old tale, known to author.

"Are you sleeping": and other two verses can be found in *Songfest*, by Dick and Beth Best (New York: Crown Pub., 1948, 1955).

"Little Boy Blue": AMG.

"Adieu!": cited in *Early New England Gravestone Rubbings* by Edmund Vincent Gillon, Jr. (New York: Dover, 1966).

"Ding, dong bell": AMG.

"Jane, Joan": is a fabrication of the author's based on an old nursery rhyme.

"The Leith police": AMG.

"He who eats": cited in "In the Proverbial Stew," *Boston Globe*, Section B (Sunday, July 6, 1975).

"The sailors say": AMG.

"A chieftain to": in *The Literary Ballad* by Anne Harvey Ehrenpreis (Columbia, S.C.: University of South Carolina Press, 1966).

"O, for a capful": AMG.

"Milkman, milkman": AMG.

"Orlando Gibbons": all Gibbons quotes from the "London Street Cries" song from *Elizabethan & Jacobean Ayres, Madrigals and Dances* by the New York Pro Musica (Decca Records, DL 9406).

"In Russia soul cakes": cited in *Standard Dictionary of Folklore, Mythology and Legend* edited by Maria Leach (New York: Funk & Wagnall, 1972).

"Dame get up": AMG.

"Christmas is coming": AMG.

"Under the greenwood tree": "As You Like It," Act II, Scene V; from *The Complete Works of William Shakespeare, The Cambridge Editions Text*, edited by William Aldis Wright (Garden City Books, 1936).

"Midsummer's eve": AMG.

"Riddles from": *The Girl's Own Book* by Mrs. Child (London: Thomas Tegg & Son, 1837).

"The kookaburra": *The World Book Encyclopedia*.

"Three hundred years ago in Peking": cited in "Strange But True" column in *True* magazine, in author's collection.

"The Chinese immortal": cited in *Standard Dictionary of Folklore, Mythology and Legend*.

"Donkey, donkey": AMG.

"My heart's in the Highlands": Robert Burns, *Burns* (Chicago: M. A. Donohue & Co., 1907).

"Field mice": *The New York Times*, in author's collection.

"Oh father": retold from *The Fables of Aesop*, edited by Joseph Jacobs (New York and London: Macmillan, 1894).

"The Sun was shining": from *Through the Looking Glass*, by Lewis Carroll (New York: Random House, 1946).

"Wake up, Jacob": from *The Fireside Book of Children's Songs*, by Marie Winn (New York: Simon & Schuster, 1966).

"Oh, slowly, slowly": saying in author's family.

"Work as though": cited in *Simple Gifts: The Story of the Shakers* by Jane Yolen (New York: Viking, 1976).

"Fare thee well": old song known by author.

Alphabetical List of Rounds

All Is Silent, 84–85
All Things Must Perish, 6

Bell Doth Toll, The, 16–17
Boat, a Boat, A, 58–59
Buy My Dainty Fine Beans, 70–71

Canoe Round, 60–61
Chairs to Mend: I, 64
Chairs to Mend: II, 66–67
Cherries So Ripe, 69
Christmas Is Coming, 76–77
Come Follow, Follow, 78–79

Dame, Lend Me a Loaf, 74–75
Dona Nobis Pacem, 112–113
Donkeys and Carrots, 92

Early to Bed, 26–27

French Cathedrals, 38–39
Frère Jacques, 42–43
Frogs, The, 100

Ghost of John, The, 46–47
Goodnight to You All, 106–107
Great Tom Is Cast, 21

Hey Ho, Nobody's Home, 30–31
Hey Ho, to the Greenwood, 96–97
Ho, Ev'ry Sleeper Waken, 104–105

Jack, Boy, Ho!, 48–49
Jane Glover, 50–51

Kookaburra, 86–87

Little Bells of Westminster, 20

Make New Friends, 11
Man's Life's a Vapor, 28
Merrily, Merrily, 12–13
My Dame Hath, 52

Now We'll Make the Rafters Ring, 10

Oh, How Lovely Is the Evening, 22–23
Oh, Music, Sweet Music, 8

Rose, Rose, 24–25
Rounds About Rounds, 114
Row, Row, Row Your Boat, 56

Sandy McNab, 54–55
Scotland's Burning, 36
Seven Great Towns of Greece, 34–35
Shaker Life, 108–109
Shalom Chaverim, 110
Soul Cakes, 72–73
Summer Is A-Coming In, 80–82
Sun It Rises, The, 102
Sweetly Sings the Donkey, 94–95

Thou Poor Bird, 88
Three Blind Mice, 98–99
Turn Again, Whittington, 40–41

Viva la Musica, 14

Where Are You Going?, 62
Where Is John?, 44–45
White Coral Bells, 18–19
White Sand and Gray Sand, 68
Why Shouldn't My Goose, 90–91
Wise Men Were but Seven, The, 32–33

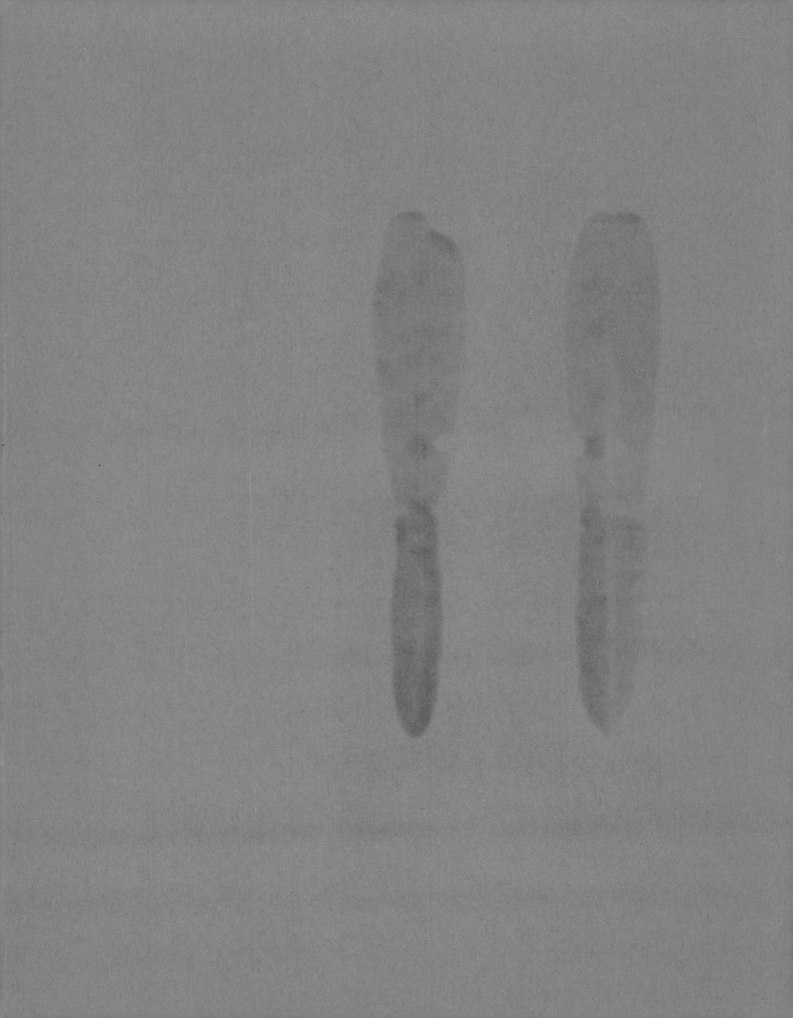